Ralf Peters

A Little Book of Voice

Ralf Peters

A Little Book of Voice

translated by Agnes Pollner
and Gabriele Reifenberg

Bibliografische Information der Deutschen Nationalbibliothek:
Die Deutsche Nationalbibliothek verzeichnet diese Publikation
in der Deutschen Nationalbibliografie; detaillierte bibliografische
Daten sind im Internet über http://dnb.dnb.de abrufbar.

@2017 Ralf Peters
Herstellung und Verlag:
BoD – Books on Demand, Norderstedt

ISBN: 9783744896344

I have to struggle with the people I want to teach. Their main argument against me is: "You just have to take me as I am!" (…) But what I have to tell them is that they will not dissuade me from seeing them richer than they think themselves to be.

Alfred Wolfsohn

for Maja Dentan

Introduction

Since about the turn of the millennium the subject of the human voice has moved beyond the purely artistic and therapeutic fields into business training studies and colleges of further education. Business groups and associations focus increasingly on vocal communication as one of the major aspects of everyday business life. As a result, vocal training regularly features in Companies' in-house performance enhancement programmes. The vocal training offered needs to rise to meet this challenge. Until now voice teachers have mainly focussed on training singers or on working with diction, either for professional speakers or as speech therapy. Now they are suddenly faced with a brand new clientele with no genuine interest in voice itself, wishing only to make better use of their voices in business contexts, and in more effectively controlling their voice in negotiations or conferences. At the same time, training requirements may sometimes be quite unspecific like "doing something for the voice". This may seem a reasonable request. But will it be adequately achieved through exercises and training that have been designed mainly for singers, radio announcers or speech therapists?

In 2005 I was faced with this question for the first time when I was asked to create vocal training modules for use in a business context. At that time I was not sure if I could come up with something that would give participants anything of value to use in their jobs. Although my own training as a Roy-Hart-voice teacher has been quite extensive – one of our main directions being the exploration of the full range of the voice beyond conventional singing and speech – up to that point my activities had been more or less focussed on the artistic field. After giving the first vocal training course in a business context I had doubts. After many more courses I am still asking myself how to design a vocal training programme that does not have artistic or therapeutic objectives as its aim. The following thoughts and comments in this booklet on voice investigate this question. Writing this I am not interested in stereotypical answers but wish to provide my readers with food for thought. That is why I am presenting my musings in the form of a sketchbook of written fragments which may well overlap and repeat themselves. If my writing inspires any of my colleagues to further clarify their own concepts on vocal work, this would indeed be a very welcome result. The non-expert but interested reader, on the other hand, might intuit by reading the following pages how much there is to discover by learning about the voice, even though they may not wish to use it artistically in any way.

This text is not intended as a booklet of instructions on how to give voice training. No exercises – with one exception – are presented. My reason for this is that professionals already have lots of exercises up their sleeves and newcomers will, in my opinion, be much better off receiving their first vocal exercise in person with a teacher, rather than reading it up in a book. In writing this booklet, my intention is to provide a possible framework for developing vocal programmes with non-artists. My ideas on this subject are related to the thoughts and practices of Alfred Wolfsohn and Roy Hart. I have expounded their views and working concepts elsewhere. If reading this booklet sparks off interest in the Wolfsohn / Roy Hart approach to voice, it would be a very welcome outcome.

Free play of the voice versus technique and tricks

The first thing I do when introducing my course: "Voice in professions" is to ask the participants about their expectations: what do they wish to achieve by means of the voice work? What usually comes up first is that somebody says they would like to know tips and tricks to improve their voice or to work it more effectively. There are of course efficient ways to, for instance, make a voice hold out better in a difficult situation, and I am very happy to pass them on. But I don't in actual fact believe in tricks, and for some people this might initially come as a disappointment. The reason why I don't believe in tricks is that even if you are vocally very proficient, tricks in a moment of vocal crisis are only successful if you are able to allow your voice sufficient freedom to apply them. But if a voice already possesses this kind of freedom or free play it doesn't need tricks to sustain itself. It is this very freedom that enables a voice to respond in a flexible and open way to all kinds of challenges, choosing its own route and whatever support it needs by itself.

Voice as partner

When I discuss voice with artists and non-artists in my classes I am regularly faced with the deeply-rooted assumption that the human voice is a sort of instrument or tool. Such an attitude certainly has its benefits. Once you are more familiar with your instrument and know how to use it to best effect you will certainly be able to play the vocal instrument or apply the vocal tool better. There are some aspects in understanding the voice as an instrument that harmonize quite well with our attitude towards it and that might turn out to be quite helpful. However the drawback concerning the image of the voice as an instrument or tool is that in focusing on an attitude like this the extensive capacities inherent in the human voice are greatly diminished. By highlighting the mechanical logic of the instrument as an outer object you relate to the implication is that by perfecting techniques of breath, speech and singing a person will be able to learn how to make best use of the mechanics of the voice, and that they will master their voice through working every part of the vocal apparatus most effectively.

We are not arguing against the fact that there are more and less effective ways of using the voice in speech or singing. There are. What we are proposing here is a radical shift in the overall attitude towards the voice.

Can we conceive of a communication between an individual and his or her vocal expression well-informed and intimate enough to give the voice the freedom to choose by itself the most adequate technique for its development? In that way I and my voice could interact without effort to completely tune into whatever a situation requires unimpeded by a heavy load of sophisticated know-how about physiology and educational theory.

By choosing to train and develop the voice in a particular way the specific training methods employed will inevitably emphasise certain aspects of the voice over others in order to successfully achieve a proposed vocal standard. As a result problems will occur further along the line. It is a well-known fact that a significant number of singing students have, by the time they graduate, not only not enhanced their quality of singing but find that the quality of their singing has diminished and that they do not enjoy singing any more. Expert knowledge has its value but in my experience the voice has the capacity to know how to do things best by itself. You only need to ask your voice. Thinking of your voice as an instrument, however, gives you no partner to address your question to.

As long as you keep relating to your voice as an instrument or tool certain aspects concerning the relationship between a human being and their voice will remain hidden. When you don't need it any longer you put the instrument or tool away, and you stay separated until you need it again and take it up. Your voice on the other hand stays with you always even if you don't make sounds. This simple fact demonstrates that the voice is not like an instrument or an object that you pick up, put to use and put away. Your voice is part of you in a very specific way and in that respect not at all like a violin and even less like a screwdriver. Your voice is not a thing. It is integral to your being and doesn't exist apart from you. And yet it is possible to distance yourself from it in a way. Otherwise you wouldn't be able to talk about it. Dissociating from it in that way does not necessarily imply a concept of hierarchy as would be implied when the metaphor of the instrument is used. Regarding an instrument or tool there is a clear definition of who uses what: I am using the instrument for a certain purpose. Positions are not interchangeable in the relationship between the instrument and me. It will always be me performing an action, using the tool or instrument to complete that action. Hierarchically my position must be, by definition, superior to that of the instrument.

My voice, in contrast, is equipped to act quite independently and it does so, as often as not against my very ideas and objectives. Delicate or agitated situations often cause the voice to act independently, doing what it wants to do instead of meeting my expectations. Your voice may not take orders, acting instead in a wilful manner you wouldn't expect from a mere instrument. In situations like these the voice represents not simply a problem to be solved. By its specific way of expressing itself the voice directly comments on the actual situation and is an indicator of changes that are occurring and need responding to. Incorporating that information you are relating to your voice as a partner and not in a hierarchical way. Voice as a partner is informing you through its modulation about the situation you are in, internally and externally, reflecting back to you your feelings and condition. When we adopt the view of partnership, so-called vocal problems (i. e. the voice becoming tight, too high, too thin, trembling, shaking) can be understood as signals precisely indicating approaching dangers or risks in communicative situations. Your voice is able to anticipate a shift of atmosphere much sooner than your consciousness. By listening to its signals your capacity to respond to shifts and changes even before they become manifest will increase. Voice as an acoustically expressive partner will allow you a degree of flexibility in communication that would not be accessible to you otherwise. Real, i. e. chronic, problems or limitations of the voice manifest when those signals the voice is transmitting are constantly ignored or misunderstood. As a consequence they transform into vocal habits or mannerisms that may turn into vocal dysfunctions or even inflict damage to the vocal organs. At that point we rush to see speech therapists or even surgeons – most of them devotees to the logic of repairing a failing instrument. Therefore what liberating the voice to be itself means is learning to listen to your own voice and to meet it in an unprejudiced and direct way. By respecting your voice in that way you are giving it the space to link into smooth cooperation with yourself, diminishing causes for irritation and disturbance.

Listening to your voice as a partner means first and foremost not judging but interpreting. This is the crucial point in developing the voice from our point of view.

Judging a vocal expression as right or wrong, adequate or inadequate, as too loud, too soft, too harsh or too delicate, or with any other parameter of criticism one might have (one tends to be quite inventive in that respect) restricts the scope of the human voice and obstructs its liberation and free movement.

Notes

Having looked at the concept of developing and liberating the voice in my classes I introduce the diagram below, designed by myself (the basic idea being much older, I believe), to now focus on the subject of "voice and communication". The parameters of the 'triangle of contact' describe communicative situations that require the use of the voice.

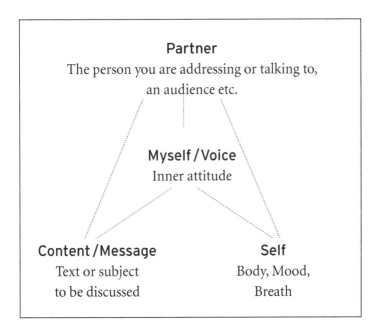

Partner
The person you are addressing or talking to, an audience etc.

Myself / Voice
Inner attitude

Content / Message
Text or subject
to be discussed

Self
Body, Mood,
Breath

Whenever you are giving a lecture or presenting a paper in a team, talking to a client, customer or patient, your part as the speaker – simplifying it somewhat – manifests in three aspects of contact:

– The person or group you are addressing or talking to, those you pass your message on to.
– The content of your talk, lecture or paper.
– And you yourself.

The first two aspects are quite obvious; the third tends to be overlooked or to be ignored altogether most of the time. In communicative situations the three points of the triangle – audience, content and you – resonate with each other. If the energy exchange between you and the three points is balanced, you are in a flow. But your response to them could also be either too weak or too strong. What do we mean by that?

Contact with the audience is too weak if a speaker who presumably wishes to convey a message doesn't in fact act in such a way that he is heard and understood by his audience. He or she will hide behind the lectern or their notes, will speak with a deadpan voice, never really turning towards the people next to or in front of them (for fear of a mistake or slip of tongue), thus making true communication impossible. As a result the party being addressed will literally feel not addressed and will not have heard or understood what the person wanted to say.

Contact with the audience is too strong when the speaker's wish to entertain takes precedence over the content. In the end everybody will be quite enthusiastic about the person (including the speaker him- or herself) and at the same time nobody will be able to remember what was actually said. In such a case being too strongly focussed on pleasing the audience will obstruct contact with the message or the topic of the talk.

The reason for weak contact with the topic of a lecture is in most cases a quite trivial one: lack of preparation. Only when you know exactly what you are talking about will your subject matter be well received by your audience. The better you know the material the more you will be able to talk about it in a lively and interesting manner. Feeling insecure and uncertain about the topic will increase the need to hang on to the fixed script and put pressure on the voice. When you are giving a talk there may be open questions or unsolved problems around the subject under discussion. There is no need to hush them up or avoid problematic areas. It is on the contrary quite important to know as much as possible about the questions and problems that might come up.

Examples of over-involvement with content at the expense of contact with one's listeners will probably readily spring to mind for those readers who went to university. Who hasn't experienced lectures where the male lecturer, or more rarely female, is so bound up with their subject that contact with their student listeners seems to threaten a disturbance of their self-involved train of thought.

When we are afraid of exactly those disturbances that might challenge our concepts we tend to overly involve ourselves with the subject. In the end nothing at all will be communicated.

Contact with myself in a communicative situation – a potentially schizophrenic affair as it seems – takes place on various levels: on the immediate physical level, on the level of the breath and voice and on the level of one's disposition.

While lecturing will I be able to be aware of the position of my body and my posture? Can I feel the contact between the ground and the soles of my feet? Do I allow gravity to act on my body to keep it well grounded? Or will agitation and nervousness cause me to be pulled up and lifted off my feet?

Agitation and excitement tend to push your energies upwards. Observing other speakers you may have noticed how excitement literally lifts people off the ground, making them stand on their toes or on one leg only. Obviously this puts you in a very unstable and fragile position so that any small thing might easily blow you off your feet. If you are susceptible to agitated states I recommend practising grounding before and during your talk, taking care to let the weight of the body sink through into the feet and have full contact with the ground.

If your energy has a tendency to move upwards in exciting or demanding situations this will also affect your voice. You may have noticed how in certain difficult moments your voice inadvertently rose in pitch, felt constricted, broke, became fainter or closed down completely; it might have grown husky or croaky and you felt a sudden prickling in your throat. Difficulties like these usually can be avoided by training to be aware of minimal shifts in your voice and by responding to them through grounding yourself in the body as suggested above. You need to centre yourself right in that moment and allow yourself a gap to exhale deeply. It is a strong indication that you are in danger of losing yourself and your voice when you notice that your breath is growing shallow or when you feel a tendency to hold your breath instead of releasing it; now you better take action to ground yourself in your body immediately.

We shouldn't think of vocal and physical responses to stressful situations as isolated random occurrences. They are closely linked to movement within the psyche. Such movement provokes an inner shift or impulse for adjustment. The inner situation corresponds to the outer and at the same time to the atmosphere between individuals in a certain space. The outer atmosphere in which you find yourself affects your mood or psychic tuning; vice versa your actions and impulses affect the atmosphere. By training to be clearly aware of inner and outer atmospheres, by learning to be guided by them and at the same time being aware of your own influence on them, a freedom of play will arise allowing the voice to move about freely and to respond easily to any changes that may occur in the outer and inner situation.

Finally, just as discussed above when referring to contact with the audience or the subject matter, contact with yourself may also be too fixed or too loose. When you are too loosely connected with yourself you will not be able to stay „with yourself"; you are prone to lose yourself in a situation or in your emotions and as a consequence it will be quite obvious to others that you are not master in your own home. You will also be in danger of losing yourself if you worry too much about the slightest vocal or physical impulses or movements while talking or lecturing. Being overly attentive to yourself will make it increasingly difficult to keep in touch with the audience or to stay linked to the subject you are talking about.

Each of the three points of contact highlight important areas concerning your communication and it is vital to aim at a healthy and lively balance between them. Once you are well balanced try to keep the balance stable as much as you can. Here the quality of vitality is another key element: a stable and lively balance relies on the ability to counterbalance and compensate at any given point during your lecture. There is no such thing as perfect balance as a fixed state. Balance means movement and continuous change. At one moment you might need to relate more to the audience, in the next you might need to touch in again with yourself and one second later it is the topic that needs your attention.

The triangle of contact is a basic formula and as such needs more elaboration to analyse specific situations such as, for instance, lecturing together with a partner where keeping contact with that person will strongly affect what is going on.

The triangle of contact is used as a device to analyse and understand lectures or conversations we reconstruct in my classes. It makes it easy to spot and specify potential imbalances in communication.

An anecdote about Husserl: The lively discussion

Whenever I introduce the triangle of contact in my classes I like to tell the following anecdote. It illustrates quite nicely what it could mean to be too strongly fixed on the content of your talk.

In the 1920ties and 30ties Edmund Husserl, the founder of modern phenomenology, was teaching philosophy in Freiburg. The nowadays much better known Martin Heidegger was one of his assistants at that time. Heidegger reports how at the beginning of a certain tutorial Husserl invites his students to put forward and discuss with him whatever questions they have. The first question is asked and answering it Husserl launches himself into a 90-minute monologue. This completely fills up the scheduled time for the tutorial and so Husserl and Heidegger walk back to their office together. Says Husserl: "That was a very lively discussion this afternoon, don't you think?"

Quite an explicit example for someone who forgets about the world, others and himself by completely drowning in the subject.

Everyone operating in the field of communication training knows the 'JoHari Window'. It is called 'JoHari' after its creators, the psychologists Joseph Luft and Harry Ingham. Their 'window' displays four discrete aspects of communication dealing with how evident these aspects are to either the speaker or the audience or both. My version of the window for the voice derives from that. It operates in a similar way arriving at slightly different results.

Like theirs my version is divided into four areas.

The first area is the open aspect of the voice that is directly perceptible for both the person using their voice and the listener. In this area there are no secrets, everything is present and evident in an open way.

The second area in my version is called the 'deaf spot' corresponding to the much better-known 'blind spot' of the original JoHari window. The deaf spot indicates the specific part of my voice that I myself am not able to hear. This has to do with the strange fact that only I myself in the whole world am able to hear my own voice in the way I do. Every other being capable of hearing will not hear my voice as I do. This fact is a fairly recent discovery, made only 150 years ago. It emerged along with the invention of the phonograph. For the first time in history the phonograph made it possible to hear one's own voice from the 'outside'. When we are speaking or singing we hear our own voice from the inside via the bones as well as from the outside via the ears. This combination of inner and outer hearing creates a specific blend of sound perception that is clearly distinct from any other acoustic events that are merely perceived from the outside and almost exclusively by the ears. Obviously when you hear a recording of your own voice you are hearing your voice now from the outside and with your ears only. This is a major shift of perception in relation to your own voice. Today people tend to mistake the outer perception of their voice as the 'objectively' or impartially correct one. People hearing their recorded voice automatically assume that what they hear in this way is what their voice 'really' sounds like. But there is no such thing as objective or impartial hearing!

The third area of the window concerns the restrained aspect of the voice. In many communicative situations, and probably quite frequently when they are job-related, we hold back certain moods, emotions or impulses that we are experiencing. Expressing them – vocally or physically – doesn't seem appropriate to the situation. Emotion, as is often stated, shouldn't interfere with the purpose of a meeting or lecture. That is why participants in voice classes often express a wish to learn to be able to restrain the emotional and sometimes so irritatingly interfering part of their voice – and will be disappointed. I don't teach that.

When we are listening to a voice under a strain as implied above it is a striking fact that the restraint itself is clearly audible to others. After some training it will be audible to ourselves too. Our acoustic sensorium is highly sensitive and capable of perceiving in great detail what is vocally conveyed. Not only do we sense that there is something wrong but also that the voice in question is hiding something. When listening to a restrained voice we usually start to feel vaguely uncomfortable. We can't really say what it is that makes us feel like that or why. But clearly we don't want to go on listening to that voice and we will try to wriggle out of the situation as best we can. When training to develop the voice we are working to ease that area of restraint and by this gradually to allow more openness into the vocal expression. This will invite others to be just as open in return.

The fourth area of the window of vocal communication deals with the repressed or unconscious aspects resonating in a voice, aspects somebody will be more or less unaware of (this would be the blind spot area of the JoHari window). These vocal aspects are distinct from the restrained area as they are to a large extent not acknowledged and therefore not on the agenda as something to be restrained. Repressed aspects are not directly accessible to us because we – as one might argue – succeed only too well in hiding them from ourselves and the world. But the effort involved leaves its trace in a voice and is again clearly audible. Learning to listen to your own voice closely and with a friendly attitude will allow repressed vocal aspects to be retrieved. The Roy Hart development of voice is based on such a strategy of deep listening underpinned by decades of experiential know-how. The key situation of our voice work is the dialogic exchange between one individual using their voice and another listening to it. In this way, through a shared process of growing awareness, we gradually free the voice to be itself.

When teaching in a group situation we take advantage of the potential of shared feedback to track down unconscious aspects of the voice. Images, thoughts, emotions or memories sparked off in others while listening to a voice often reveal the key to a blocked vocal area.

Vocal Window of Communication

– a diagram subdividing the different meaningful sound aspects of the voice in communication.

Open Aspect Aspects of my voice overtly audible to myself and others.	*Deaf Spot* Aspects of my voice not audible to myself i. e. because I am hearing my own voice in a specific way, differently from everybody else.
Restrained Parts Vocal aspects I don't want to express or expose in a certain situation. The restraint and the effort involved is audible for others.	*Repressed or* *unconscious Parts* Vocal aspects being expressed without my being aware of it, i. e. emotional colouring or unconscious messages that listeners pick up and respond to.

There is no such thing
as 'objective' hearing

One of my standard exercises in beginners' classes is to ask the participants to describe their own voice to a partner. People are often puzzled by this request or feel apprehensive, thinking they might not be able to describe it correctly. During the feedback following this partner exercise participants often discuss how strange and unfamiliar people perceive the sound of their own voice when they hear it recorded, for instance on an answering machine, and played back to them. Statements like these seem to imply the assumption that the voice as heard from the outside is what the sound of a voice objectively or truly is. If you are hearing your voice in that way you are therefore supposedly hearing it as it truly is because everybody else is hearing it that way. This suggests that you yourself will never hear the true sound of your own voice because you are hearing it inwardly and this is supposedly not what your voice really sounds like. If you are hearing your voice in that way you are therefore supposedly hearing it as it truly is because everybody else is hearing it that way. What this suggests is that you yourself will never be capable of hearing the true sound of your own voice because you never will hear it just from outside but always in addition inwardly.

In this notion a combination of mistakes and misunderstandings meet. As mentioned above, mankind never knew about this issue until 150 years ago, when techniques to record and play back voices started to develop. Before that time, how would you know that you are hearing your own voice in a different way than every other living being? Do we therefore assume that in the time before the invention of the phonograph people weren't able to judge the effect of their voice as exactly as we do now that we are able to hear our voice from the outside? Most probably they could.

What is it we hear when we are hearing ourselves from the outside? It is only the individual listening ear that can provide an answer. The individual listening ear carries with it a whole history of listening, just like the voice does. Your ear and hearing is unique in exactly the same way as your voice is and both are subject to constant transformation. If you listen to a recording of your voice today and then again in ten years time you won't hear the same thing. Today certain facets of the voice might sound peculiar or attractive to you but might be completely ignored by your ear later on. I know this from my own experience.

In my early years as a radio announcer I used to listen to recordings of my voice quite regularly to keep track of mistakes and to be able to correct them. This was by no means an easy task. Like many people I didn't particularly like the sound of this unfamiliar voice – supposedly mine – blasting out of the recorder. When I listened to the same recordings many years later I perceived my voice quite differently, appreciating its divers qualities to a greater extent. The recording hadn't changed but I and my ear had.

Every person has his or her own historical or biographical imprint on their capacity to hear. But people with similar social backgrounds will most probably hear similar things. Their voices will sound more alike in comparison with voices of people from different cultures or parts of society. Although in the same society there may be quite distinct modes of conditioning; we will find that there is always play between cultural and individual aspects. And each individual in a group will hear a voice with their individual ear in their own specific way. There is no such thing as impartial or objective hearing. That's what makes getting feedback from others about your voice so illuminating. It demonstrates how others perceive all kinds of diverse facets of sound in one and the same voice. What is audible to us in our own voice is only a fraction of the actual richness perceived by others.

Voice Development with Body, Mind and Soul

Freeing the voice to be itself can be accessed from various levels. If you follow the European classification you access it via body, mind and soul. (This classification is at least as much a result of convention as it is of insight. Where do we draw the line between the three areas? Where does the body begin and the soul end? And where does mind come in? Asian systems – just to give one example – classify thinking as a perception.)

Vocal events are events of the body. No voice without a body. Physical states influence the voice directly. A tired person's voice is different from that of a rested, alert one. Posture also has a bearing on the voice, as well as physical tension and, of course, breathing. We have the capacity to become aware of all these aspects. By training to be aware of physical actions and reactions while speaking or using your voice you will learn to use all kinds of physical states transforming them into support for the voice.

On the physical level producing vocal sound is a muscular process. With training the muscles involved this process will become more flexible and stronger. Training the voice on the physical level doesn't imply that we need to know in detail which muscle is working where and how when we are singing or speaking. The voice is trained simply by opening up, alive and ready, to those vocal possibilities it is able to access easily.

In the same way the sound of a voice is informed by the different psychic aspects of your being – moods, emotions, desires or fears. Your mood in any given situation will colour the timbre of the voice. Furthermore your voice will display which aspects of your emotional setup are given permission to thrive and what you are holding back. This is predominantly an unconscious process. Listening to the voice together deeply allows access to this area. The sharing of feedback between the person who has used their voice and the listeners is potentially insightful and instructive.

Concepts, ideas and thought patterns, judgments and assessment criteria: the mind in all its aspects has an enormous effect on my ability to conceive possibilities in my voice. If the vision for my voice is narrow it will be difficult for me to free it without having removed the mental blockage first. That's why talking about the phenomenon of the human voice and its wide potential plays an important part in teaching voice especially in classes with non-artists. Often when old thought patterns are dissolved a direct vocal liberation is stimulated opening up vocal ranges that hadn't been heard for many years or never before at all.

Freeing the Voice to be itself

Nowadays professional daily routine consists mainly in following and accomplishing external requirements or standards developed for your professional activity by whomever and in whatever way. Therefore when working on the development of the voice it is essential to make sure concepts like these don't exert too much influence. The voice work we are presenting here is not about vocal improvement, efficacy or any such thing. Our intention is to liberate the voice to be itself. To accomplish that the voice does not need to learn anything additional. It is rather a question of unlearning certain habits and concepts about the voice so that it regains its freedom of movement in the vocal field. The voice already knows how to do whatever is needed. We only need to grant it the freedom to unfold. This however may be hard work and quite an open-ended process. An ultimately liberated voice is an ideal; cultural influence and personal history shape it into human size. A voice that is comfortable in itself knows about its freedom and limitations. It is naturally supportive for the (professional) life of the person accommodating it.

Voice and Breath

Again and again I am asked in my classes about the correct way of breathing. In my experience it is necessary to be quite cautious about this area. Training in the so-called correct way to breathe (whatever that means there being innumerable, mutually contradictory schools of breathing) often causes people to fixedly control their breath only allowing certain breathing movements that they deem to be the correct ones. Even though it is a good idea to give everyone the opportunity to get to know abdominal breathing, the crucial point consists of learning to set the breath free. Breath, in the same way as voice, knows best how to move in any given situation once you allow it freedom. Breathing freely instead of correctly! Just as developing the voice is all about allowing the vocal field to come alive, the breathing exercises I teach aim at opening the respiratory spaces in such a way that the breath can move freely of its own volition.

My Voice

The possessive pronoun 'my' linked to voice can have various kinds of meaning. Someone who lacks experience in terms of voice will claim the most familiar part of his voice as 'his' or belonging to him. If this person suddenly experiences his voice uttering as yet unknown sounds in class his first reaction will be something like: "This is not my voice" or "That is not me". And yet every vocal sound my voice is capable of producing is obviously part of my voice and therefore of me. The task of developing the voice consists precisely in integrating all these vocal sounds, finally arriving at an inner attitude that comprehends them all as being part of me. In that context the term 'authentic' is a potentially problematic one. Course participants may reject new and unfamiliar vocal sounds because their ears don't accept them as 'authentic'. But authenticity is not the same as familiarity. If it were, there would be no development leading into new and unknown areas. Roy Hart's teacher, Alfred Wolfsohn, used to say: "I take the liberty of hearing and seeing more of you than you do just now."

<u>Notes</u>

The Three Elements of the Voice

When we are focussing on the tonality of the human voice, for the moment leaving aside the aspects of speech intonation, rhythm etc., we find that every vocal sound consists of three elements. It contains a certain pitch, volume and colouring or timbre. The parameters of pitch and volume, in addition to being audible, are also quite easy to quantify in units of decibel and hertz. The third element, the vocal colouring, can't be pinpointed so easily. In my classes I often use the framework of these components to develop further insight into the voice, linking them to the discussion of personal, cultural and practical aspects.

a) Tone Pitch and Vocal Pitch: high and low Voices
Every single vocal sound has a well defined pitch in tone and every voice has its own vocal pitch, a certain range where that voice operates comfortably without effort. This vocal pitch or natural range seems to be a genetic disposition. The technical term is neutral setting, neutral pitch or 'Indifferenzlage'. It is the natural, effortless pitch of your voice, the range where your voice feels at ease. In day-to-day use however many voices are set too high for a comfortable or natural pitch. The reason for that may not come as a surprise: accumulated inner tension directly affects the voice. A number of voice therapists have created various exercises for finding your natural or comfortable pitch and you might like to experiment with them to find the right one for you. One of them suggests visualizing yourself relaxing in a deck chair: there is nothing to do, the person next to you is telling you a nice, unspectacular story and you grunt ascent with a relaxed 'mmhm'. The sound of

this minimal vocal utterance is most probably located at your most effortless pitch. When I refer to this whole subject area in my training I do it mostly to demonstrate that there is the possibility of using your voice with almost no effort at all. My preferred approach however consists of listening to the strained pitch or vocal range that a voice displays and to then explore together with the person involved why it has settled in that particular range. When we realize what a shift upwards in vocal pitch might signify and what effect it has on the sound of our voice, it will be much easier to let go of the habitual effort and to let the voice move to a more comfortable place. Obviously a process like that can't be accomplished in a brief seminar. A deeper involvement with the voice over a longer period of time will be necessary.

It is not necessarily only the pitch of a voice that gives the impression of a voice as high or low. It also depends on how many high or low aspects of a voice are allowed to resonate freely and are therefore an audible part of the speaking voice. A low voice in which also high aspects resonate creates a clear, awake and open impression. A high voice with low aspects sounds engaging, mature, experienced – to name just a few possibilities. Herein lies a major goal of my voice work: to awaken the tonal diversity of the voice in order to enhance the 'normal' speaking voice with additional facets. There is no point in initiating highly intensive voice training when working with people who are not artistically interested in the voice. It is much more a question of working towards integrating the higher and lower registers that are easily accessible into the existing range of the voice. Initially instances of timidity, resistance or self-consciousness may occur but they are generally overcome quite quickly. Hereby the voice coach serves as an important role model when he or she demonstrates a natural ease in using the whole diversity and range of the human voice.

b) Volume

It is not so easy to achieve a variation in the volume of the voice that is without undue effort. We have a very fine ear for how much vocal volume is socially acceptable or not, and when we are transgressing these boundaries. In addition to that, social occasions where you are free to just let your voice go out as loudly as you wish are becoming scarce in our present society. In the football stadium or at other sporting events are the exception here. (Although in the younger generation things seem to be improving; nowadays people tend to sing more than in the last 40 to 50 years.)

Producing volume without straining the voice is only possible when I am connected to the emotional situation I am experiencing. I will be able to get louder much more easily if I invoke an atmosphere or a situation that requires greater vocal volume from me. It is also necessary to stay grounded in the body. When we are training to increase the vocal volume exercises focus on opening inner spaces, activating the belly and at the same time letting go of tension.

c) Vocal Colouring or Timbre

This is the most complex of the three elements. Unlike the other two parameters timbre can't be measured like them and evades precise definition. (In the most current modern music for instance composers work with the concept that pitch is nothing else than another tonal mode.) When we are talking about the timbre of a voice we are considering its vocal colour. And this is a visual term where we as visual beings have a much broader vocabulary at our disposal than that of the acoustic field. The colour or timbre of the voice is what makes a voice unique. Every voice has its specific sound. It is created by the particular mixture of tonal colouring that is audible in a voice. The basic blend of a timbre makes a voice recognisable and it is this specific blend of colour that will be transformed by changes in the inner or outer situation of a person.

When we work on their voices with actors we train them to consciously transform their vocal colouring or timbre according to the emotional situation or the demands of the character. Alfred Wolfsohn developed a very effective exercise to enhance this skill. When you focus on different places in the body and let the voice resonate from there the vocal colouring moves into very distinct characteristics of timbre. The beginners' version discriminates between sounds that are based predominantly in the head, those in the upper and lower chest region and those that are based in the belly or the pelvis. This idea is potentially expandable as much as one likes. It is a most helpful exercise when we intend to explore the entire field of the human voice. But I also use it in classes with non-artists in order to communicate the huge potential of the variation obtainable within one's range of vocal colouring or timbre.

How to work with People who have no specific interest in the voice?

Mostly my training 'voice in the professions' is offered by companies to their employees in the context of in-house training and as a rule participants don't book their place because of a genuine interest in the voice. They are more likely driven by the legitimate expectation that two days of vocal training will make them better equipped to do their specific jobs, that is to be able to communicate better and more effectively with customers, clients, patients and colleagues. For me this fact meant a huge challenge, especially in the beginning. How could I prove to the people in those classes that the voice itself is a fascinating subject? How could I convince them that the so much sought after improvement in efficiency would arrive naturally through the unbiased encounter with their voice and thereby cause a lasting and sustainable improvement? To aim for this outcome I chose to take the long way round. It starts with developing awareness of your own voice and from there leads you to explore how your voice actually sounds, what stories that sound evokes and finally to build a trusting relationship with your own voice. For most of the participants this is a surprising and uncommon strategy. But when they move into a practical encounter with their voice, people are soon convinced that there is a lot to discover beyond considerations of efficiency. There's a challenge in staying with one's own voice as it is in the moment and just feeling its effect and this affects even working with professionals like singing teachers, speech therapists or elocution trainers. New or up to this moment unknown vocal experiences often meet with a kind of automatic response: what is it FOR?

The core of my approach to development of the voice is in alignment with the tradition of Roy Hart and Alfred Wolfsohn and a lot could be said about it. Yet a theoretical description of the personal experience when working individually on one's voice is bound to be only be a sketchy account. The setting is completely simple. I invite a person to listen to his or her voice with my guidance for a certain length of time. We listen to the voice together without adding speech or music. I play a note on the piano (if it is not too confusing for the person working with me) and ask the person to let their voice sound that note.

This can be a new and highly unusual experience, especially for people who are not working with their voice as artists. It might trigger shyness or excitement. When we allow the 'naked' voice to emerge, we intuit at once how revealing it is about ourselves. Here the most important task of the teacher is to establish a trusting and friendly atmosphere so that the curiosity to get to know one's own voice finally outstrips the fear of being overly exposed to the listeners. But in fact when the moment of truth comes, the group is listening with an attitude of empathic solidarity. Pure vocal sounds that can't help but sound truthfully. They immediately refer the listening audience back to themselves and their own voice and leave no room for petty exposure of supposed flaws or defects.

There is no such thing as wrong notes

The development of the voice aims at uncovering the field of vocal potential and at giving the voice the most spacious room for manoeuvre possible. Therefore it doesn't know the concept of wrong notes. Any negative judgment of a vocal utterance narrows the range and free play immediately. The expansion of the vocal field correlates to building up and strengthening confidence in one's own voice. For this to succeed it is absolutely necessary that the teacher relates to each and every vocal expression of the person he or she is working with in an open, accepting and positive way. We are not saying don't try to discover new possibilities together. But when you do, it is not because there was anything wrong with what the voice displayed before; you do it only in order to explore or expand the vocal expressivity into new modes of variation.

Notes

Why do we limit our vocal field at all?

Why – so we might ask – do we normally only use a small section of our vocal possibilities and leave so many of them unused? Part of the answer is rooted in the individual person and can only be found in practical confrontation with the specific voice. But generally speaking we can distinguish between two kinds of reasons.

Every voice is limited in possibilities by the cultural conditioning a human being is born into, starting with the specific mother tongue that accentuates certain parts of the voice and neglects others through its specific sound spectrum. People who have grown up bilingually often say how they feel that speaking their different languages means speaking with different voices. Some languages use a wide range of sounds, others only a more limited segment. Some languages intersect widely in their specific sound spectrum, others don't seem to overlap in sound at all and are accordingly much more difficult to learn. However it is not only the language that usually relates to a certain culturally conditioned code but every other vocal expression as well. For insiders of a specific cultural context there is no need to spell it out. Their highly distinct rules are well known to everybody in that group. I have suggested above how that might affect the natural pitch and volume of the voice.

In addition to cultural reasons for vocal limitation there are personal reasons. It is impossible however to draw a clear distinction between the two. Your life story leaves its mark on your voice: how you spent your childhood, the people you are connected to, what you like and dislike, your fears, your talents and weaknesses, all this affects your voice strengthening certain areas and neglecting others. Often difficulties arise in a voice when the life situation of somebody changes and the habitual vocal shape does not fit in with the new situation. At such a time it might become necessary to activate parts of the voice that have been asleep for a long time. Now they need to be re-discovered as living aspects of the voice. When we look at it from this perspective it seems quite obvious that vocal development always implies an aspect of personality development. How far this process can be taken in each case depends of course on the willingness of the participant, the available time and other conditions present or missing. It is however quite evident how closely voice and psyche are connected in the vocal approach I teach.

A voice tells stories

The way somebody's voice sounds tells more than one story. It tells you something about the person, who is airing their voice, about the cultural and personal influences it was exposed to, about the current situation, about the physical and energetic state and mood they are in, and it tells us about the outer circumstances in which the voice is being deployed, about the atmosphere in the room. Every voice has a dimension in terms of cultural history and in terms of individual history; at the same time it can be read as a commentary on the current inner as well as outer situation. It is an important element of the development of the voice, as I understand it, to become aware of the stories of each individual voice, to enable them to be brought out and to be made perceptible.

Two Pillars of the Development of the Voice

Vocal development as I practise it is based on two pillars: the training of self awareness or self perception and the expansion of vocal possibilities. Vocal expansion here means the more or less trivial fact, that a free, flexible and open voice likes to be moved either in free and playful situations or in given exercises in order to activate certain segments of the voice. Training in expansion, as an element of further integration of the whole voice, in my experience works only when it is linked to the first pillar – self perception. Training to be more perceptive of myself allows me to meet my voice with interest instead of judgment and it is this alone that will enable me to make the whole potential of my vocal field available to myself in the long run. In my experience, the voice moves into the right direction of its own volition by means of attentive listening. Benevolent but acute attention to my voice seems to allow it the space to open out in width and depth.

Why discover the whole Vocal Field?

It should be sufficiently clear by now that encouraging curiosity for one's own voice is crucial to my approach and, to my mind, matters more than considerations concerning efficiency. Still, the reasonable question remains: what particular function is the discovery of the whole voice supposed to have in a business context? Some answers suggest themselves resulting from what has been said above. But in addition to that I would like to highlight a very practical effect. The wider the vocal area that is kept active and alive, the more diverse, rich and interesting the sound of a speaking voice will be. The greater diversity of timbre and the enhanced vocal range in use will gradually affect the sound of my speaking voice. Interesting speaking voices are attractive for the very reason that various different aspects resonate in them. When more tonal areas in a voice are open and alive listeners get more opportunities to enter into open communication with the person behind it.

Voice and Life

The development of the voice according to Alfred Wolfsohn and Roy Hart works on the basis of the assumption that voice and life are closely related. Voice has an effect on life and life has its effect on the voice. What seems at first sight a rather trivial observation has in fact far reaching consequences concerning insight into the voice. Discovering and integrating new room for flexibility and play in your voice will have an impact on the capacity for freedom of action in your life. And at the same time critical changes in your life situation will directly influence the possibilities of your voice. Often both processes are intertwined. In the context of a voice class a view as outlined above might at least be floated as a possibility.

Vocal flexibility instead of vocal efficiency

The development of the voice I am presenting aims to provide the voice with the freedom needed to respond with flexibility to life situations of all possible kinds. Increase of efficiency is a possible welcome side-effect but is not as such the focus of interest.

<u>Notes</u>

Voice and Hearing

Finding out more about the voice implies the inclusion of hearing. The two together form a system. Its structure is a result of their shared history. My voice can only generate the sounds (and repeat them) that I am able to hear. My hearing is shaped by what my voice is able to display. Development of the voice is for the most part an education of the ear.

Hearing: Levels of perception

There are several levels of perception to hearing. I would like to list some of them:

– the immediate evaluation of a voice: I like it or don't; it appeals to me or not, etc.
– qualities of a voice: weak, strong, friendly, aggressive, warm, cold, etc.
– relating to what's present situation: hearing excitement, joy, fear, irritation and other emotions that may have been caused by the current situation.
– biographical aspects: the life story of a person resonates in their voice; I hear and understand some of its aspects without necessarily being able to put them into words.
– mood: I hear atmospheres that emanate from a voice and they trigger an instinctive response in me. This inner response is part of hearing.
– personality: it is not only the voice I hear, but also the human being who is doing the voicing with all his or her various characteristics. On this level what I perceive is par-

ticularly dependent on my ear. The better I get to know the person who is using their voice the more their voice will change in my perception.

Perception of the voice – controlling versus observing

There is a fine line between perceiving your own voice by just being observant in an attentive way, not interfering with the process of making sounds, and on the other hand hearing it with an inner attitude of directing and controlling the voice. The difference resembles that between the evaluation and interpretation of a vocal sound. The task of the voice teacher here consists in guiding the student to become more and more sensitive to the transition from hearing that is controlling and restricting to a friendly, merely observing perception.

Four Aspects of the Development of the Voice: Using the voice, listening, feeling, thinking

The development of the voice that I am introducing here encourages four voice-related activities:
  – Using the voice: bringing movement into the voice, learning to interact with it in a playful way, activating vocal areas ready to be used that are usually not accessed in everyday life.
  – Listening: learning to listen to yourself and others without judgment, but with curiosity for the stories expressed by the tone of the voice.

– Feeling: learning to focus on the relationship between the voice and physical or psychic movement and feeling. What sentiments, emotions, physical responses go along with my voice? How are they influenced by the voice or what is their impact on the voice?
– Thinking: What do I think about my own voice and voice in general? What are my ingrained concepts or assumptions, and how could I transform these ideas in such a way that they support the process of vocal development?

Voice and Space

Voice is situated right at the point where inner and external space intersect. The two areas are interconnected. The inner space of each of the people present in a situation is linked to the others through external space. We inhale from the same space and exhale into the same space.

Vocal Tone and inner/outer Situation

Vocal tone is created by the influence of external and inner situations.

Inner Elements are:
– mental aspects concerning expectations, ideas and aims that are crucial in the present situation,
– the physical condition, physical bearing,
– the current mood.

Externally they are:
- the impact of the ambience,
- the acoustic and
- the general atmosphere in the room.

When you feel your breath vivid and alive it indicates that the exchange between inner and external space is awake.

Living Inner Space – Living Voice

A living inner space helps to achieve a living voice. The better I get to know the nooks and crannies of my inner space and integrate them, the more facets of my voice will resonate.

Notes

Acknowledgments
and further information

I am most grateful to Bettina Hesse, Karin Leyk who contributed to the publication of the German original and Angelika Kudella who layouted the German and the English version.

For the English version my gratitude goes to Agnes Pollner and Gabriele Reifenberg.

More information about my work on www.stimmfeld.de (with an english section).

On http://waystothevoice.blogspot.com my german book "Wege zur Stimme" is going to be published in english. Some chapters are already there! On stimmfeld.blogspot.de you find some of my thoughts about voice and art in english and german.

The Roy Hart International Art Centre in Malérargues / South of France has the following two websites: www.roy-hart. theatre.com with information about teachers and trainings. and www.roy-hart.com, the website for the archives maintained by Paul and Clara Silber with a collection of photos, written documents and a list of CDs and other sound documents from the time of Alfred Wolfsohn to the present day.

Printed in the USA
CPSIA information can be obtained
at www.ICGtesting.com
LVHW040802011023
759808LV00006B/197